The Art c

A Fragi............

MEMOIR
Poetry & Prose

Dorothy Alexander

Copyright © 2015 Dorothy Alexander

First Edition June 2015

All rights reserved.
No portion of this book may be reproduced in any manner
whatsoever without written permission from the publisher, except
for brief excerpts for review purposes.

Cover Photo: Author's private collection

Chapeau Rouge Editions
villagepoet1@yahoo.com

ISBN: 978-1-936923-14-4

For Arnie!
Rove On,
friend!
Dorothy
Alexander

For

My soul mate, Devey Napier

My son, Kim Andrew Alexander

My parents, Earnest & Lois Yowell

My sister, Mary Erickson, who remembers
as much as I do, but remembers it differently

My brothers, Clark, Jeff & Kevin,
who remember practically nothing

CREDO

I want to write something great but that takes time,
and I don't have much of that left. I will barely,
if at all, get done what I have set out to do today.
And that is to leave some words to remember
the route I have traveled, the trails my antecedents
took to get here. If anything is sacred, it is the path,
that we look back on, to see where we came
from, how we got to this point, to this day.

Here. Now. This moment.

FIRST FRAGMENTS

One day last year a man called me. Said his job was to investigate prospective oil and gas drilling sites to determine if such places had any historical significance. Said that one particular site revealed significant amounts of broken china and crockery fragments. Asked if I knew anything about the place, its history. It happened that the location he mentioned was my family's old farmstead where I spent my early childhood. I told him I knew plenty about it.

And I confessed then and there to breaking all those dishes and crockery!

TABLE OF CONTENTS

1.Place of Origin

2. Genealogy

3.In Media Res

4.And, Then

I.
Place of Origin

March 16, 2009, my 75th birthday, I walked 18 miles from my home in Cheyenne, Oklahoma, to the original homestead of my grandparents where I was born. Moving over the land on foot was like turning time backward. This poem came from my reflections while walking.

FRACTURED EARTH: a prophecy

1. In Media Res

Deep darkness precedes dawn and gathers
like a black cloak around an old woman
who rises from sleep and sets out walking,
as mindfully as Jeremiah on his way to prophecy
the wages of idolatry, lies, and deception.

Through a delicate fuzz of fog her steps lead
toward a grassy bank along the Lodge Pole River,
called Washita by outlanders, where it winds
around the place that Custer's Seventh Cavalry
once soaked with blood and misery.

The old woman carefully keeps to the grassy
right-of-way, wary of huge growling tractor
trucks plying roadways to and from drilling
derricks that puncture the immensity
of sky arching the grassy plain.

She places her feet in the footprints of countless
legions who walked softly from one place
to another, traversing land bridges, trudging
ever toward the edge of the known world,
disappearing over the lip of a rolling hill,
watching for things that matter: air, water, light.

She hears the trees counting their breaths, rattle
of grass rasping in the wind. She sees the white tailed
doe standing alert to ominous metallic noise, sunlight
glowing through her thin delicate ears. Faintly,
she hears the quail barking from her hidden nest,
the curlew calling down the dawn.
No longer does she hear the lesser prairie chicken
booming for its mate, nor see the antelope pivoting
on the crest of the ridge.
                            Both are gone from this place.

2.   Before Columbus

The mist of history lies thickly on the floodplain
of Washita. For time upon time, peoples passed
through or paused along this river flowing gently
from its source on the edge of the Great American
Desert to Red River, Mississippi, Gulf of Mexico,
rolling through rough broken country, flat plains,
savannahs, short-grass prairies, tall grasses, paralleled
by ribbons of timber, where people without scribes
once roamed: nomads, Athapascan, Apache, bison
hunters, farmers of maize, beans, squash, gatherers
of all stripes and inclinations. Stopping here for wood,
water, grass, game, berries, roots, nuts, all things
that ripen. Coronado stopped on his quest
for the fabled golden cities. Juan de Onate came
looking for the mythical Quivera, seeking the god
that white men worship above all things: the gold.

Old men, wise chiefs, like White Shield and Lone Wolf,
watched for these places where owls once owned the day.
They remembered what happened on each of these streams.
In the Cheyenne pattern of time everything that happens
in a place remains in that place as a part of today.

Here they heard the ululating of Monahsetah, mourning
the massacre on the Lodge Pole where the spirits moan
in agony when the yellow haired apparition drifts
on the night air. Heard, too, a low earthquake rumble
of uncountable bison trekking down the latitudes
through head high grasses before the coming of the horse.
Their thunder no longer rattles the plains.
                         The great herds are gone forever.

3. Deuteronomy

The old woman loves the past, remembers
the tears of her ancestors who walked across
these plains beside creaking wagons, the leather
of their shoes worn thin on rocky migration
making no imprint until they arrived at the place where
they stopped, made the first dugout.

Babies were born amid the dirt sifting down, settling
on the dishes, where they ate their supper on tin plates,
where mice ran down the walls as they slept.
They heard the song of the dirt everywhere.

Yellow leaves of the cottonwood fell singly
to the hard packed ground where they built the first
leaning houses from green lumber scrunched in the dryness
of long windy summers, taking to heart the chill gale of barren
winters, eating beef and bacon, and near the end of winter,
rabbits sprinkled with the last of the salt.   Finally,
the coveted patent, their names engraved by the sovereign.

4. Hard Times in the Promised Land

The blizzard of '04 howled, horses bunched
in the locust grove, cow and calf huddled
in the draw among the naked willows,
slobbers frozen like ornaments hanging
from their muzzles, chickens roosted

in the mulberries, feathers fluffed
like circus balloons, swaying in the blue
winter gale, all a matter of life and death,
living so close to the earth like children
on their mother's breast.

In time, seasons as old as the stars cycled back,
choked the rain clouds in their cribs, wound
the springs of black dust storms, smothered the seeds
of plenty like rabbits snared in a fence of pain.
The land lost all color, claimed vengeance as its own.
The wages of draught and erosion are poverty,
knuckle dragging poverty, ragged poverty, bone-aching
poverty, no-Christmas-for-kids poverty.

Always their eyes scanned the path and peripheries
of the unknown. Seeking a world without shadows.
A world where feet touched lightly on the earth,
where soft sound abounded, where deer stepped
gently among grasses, flowers, berries and mosses.
Worlds where sons and daughters came and went,
old ones passed in peace. The moon rose above
the darkling plain, stars always at their fingertips
launching messages to the night like a mother
spreading warmth among her little ones.

5.   Praise for Perseverance

The old woman's people had a passion for harsh
landscapes, for neighbors who did not depend
on modern conveniences. Those who are born to this
are held here by a thin thread, tethered, tenuous, quaking.

They have left many marks.
            But, extinction is their ultimate legacy.

Speaking clearly, if belatedly, let us honor
the fruits of the mind-bending, back-breaking
labor of their hands harvesting from million year old sod,
made flesh by the steel plow: the ears of yellow corn,
kafir's black and white grains, red seeds of maize,
straws of the broom corn, cotton boles, hand augured wells;
domestic beasts: horses, cattle, geese, guinea hens,
Leghorn chickens, Poland China hogs, barns, corrals,
henhouses, coops, sheds, smokehouses, outhouses,
root cellars, vegetable gardens near the well, orchards,
berries, black, red and blue, grapevines & grapes,
and rhubarb hitherto unknown among the buffalo chips.
                    A lingering scent of Eden.

This place seems smaller than remembered.
Flames in the distance come nearer
even as we commend ourselves for remaining,
for persevering, for holding on. Even as she asks
herself: How did the end begin? the old woman remembers
how the semen of destruction was planted
in the womb of the prairie,
                        and by what means.

6.   The Age of Petroleum

Blinded by history and hunger, most did not
Recognize the first omen of destruction
as it approached, hat in hand, buttery lies
melting in its mouth, sniffing for gold.
Like a banker in parson's clothing it came,
offering the long-awaited cornucopia,
the promise of wealth from land well-tended,
the homesteaders steadfast dream.
            Like fulfillment of biblical prophecy.

Fear of the old enemy, bone-grinding poverty
of dry-land farming in a land of dust and wind
held blindfolds in place, obscuring the coming betrayal.
Reason and caution lost in the mists of self-delusion.

Wheels of greed grind ceaselessly down roads
of wealth, power, politics and progress, paved
with lies and subterfuge, without mercy
for the natural state of the land, the blue-green planet
or the creatures who live there.

Brightness fell from the air illuminating
ambiguities of affluence, tolling the advance
of diesel fume spewing trucks, methane
in drinking water, stifling chemical smells,
leftover waste water and sludge, shattering
ancient shales deep in the earth. Ridges, hills
and plains rent asunder.

The money men came, fracking the land
                              from sea to shining sea.

7.   Lamentation

At the edge of the horizon, burned fields smolder,
smoke smudges the air like dragon breath, ashes
sift down around stacked steel derricks. Whirring
engines of defeat illuminate the path down which
the children fled, taking the meat, skin, core
and seeds with them. The old house where they
weathered decades are pulled down, razed, bulldozed.

Lilacs, mimosa, hollyhocks uprooted. The place
where you come from is like your mother. When you
no longer recognize that place, you are an orphan.

Under the dirt where big bluestem once stood
belly high to Chief Black Kettle's horse, augured
rumblings blast toxins through shattered shale,
shake the foundations of time, rattle the ancient
layers, break down the doors to the existence of life.
Hydraulic pressure applied to sands and sediment
of a once-ocean plants a toxic half-life of ten million years.
Like a mythic giant stalking the night sky, its red eyes
piercing the darkness, blinding hapless barn owls,
and all creatures that creep and crawl.

Not long ago the whisperers said where there is
smoke there is fire. Warnings were drowned
in the clink and clatter of coins dropping
from slots in the ceiling of our greed
and too much love for carnality. Now darkness
is falling. Rivers of the chromium god run deep
through the place where the tired bodies of all
who tore a living from the silence lie buried,
bones turned to glowing dust in the light of flames
from the waste pits where buffalo grass, then sweet clover,
ran in waves to the edge of evening light.

8.   Apocalypse

Rage, rage against the terrible light shadowing
the land, wind howling through a tunnel. Confront
mortality and ask again, What endures?
                              Who will bear witness?

Those who would corrupt the sacred writings
are those who would corrupt the planet,
turn the corn to ashes, gut the treasures of Eden,
barbed, brutal, straining at gnats, forcing camels
through a needle's eye, tempting imaginary

gods, fouling the nests of the young. Extinguishing
the eternal flame. By their works they shall perish.
They are not time travelers.

Nor are we.

The old woman ruefully contemplates
the impossible impasse, its inevitable outcome:
a headlong leap of the rapacious species into
the abyss of extinction. Sees the Darwinian
complicity of irony and justice restoring
natural order to the spinning green dot.

Homo Sapiens will go like the buffalo went,
but will not return like the buffalo. Evolution
will not retrace its path through Olduvai Gorge.
Humans will leave, not like a flock of blackbirds
rising, wheeling, rising again, lifting into the blue
dome, but like a black rivulet sinking into the murk.
Blinded, the wail of nothingness rippling in waves
from their mouths, they will drink the black milk
of nightfall. The day of the owl will come.

Voices will be stilled, words turned to dust,
drifting on the wind over crumbled cities
like a forgetful doze. Soon, no record will remain.
Not even one painting on a cavern wall.

See how the stars and seas and rivers in their
fragile lace of fog go on without us, morning
after morning, year after year, eon after eon.

9.   Denouement

Some steadfastly sermonized that all was wrought
by a deity sitting somewhere aloft, above the radar
of existence, a divinity rendering judgment against

too much toleration, for the sins of weakness,
poverty, or indifference.

The old woman sighs, then sniffs at hypocrisy
and feigned piety. Declares the human species
flawed ab initio. A mutant strain unable to grasp
the nature of nature. Predatory. Inadaptable.

Prone to killing each other, imagining themselves
gods, all knowing, omniscient. Their destiny, always,
extinction by their own hand.

So, like Icarus, the flawed species plunged
headlong into the sea of oblivion, into the abyss
while the blue-green earth ship sailed calmly on,
having somewhere to get to, something better to do
than watch a foolish species annihilate itself with greed.

10.   Consolation

Like Tom Sawyer sneaking back to deliciously
watch his own funeral, the old woman sees
in both directions. She peers down the millennia,
sees fracture fluid devoured by the forgiving soil,
refineries rotted into mulch under layers of dirt,
home for the sacred earthworms of tomorrow.

Sees a peaceful universe filled with space,
planets, moons, meteors and metaphors,
a tomorrow where the air is so clear
she can see the edge of the universe.

Sees a new Eden drift down in cosmic dust
they once called by the name, *God.*

(First published in Malpais Review, 2014)

OKLAHOMA

I come from a time and a place
that gives rise to song,
songs about no rain,
songs about wrongs,
about the rightness
of being
who we are,
who we were,
where we were,
and how we were.

It isn't the south with its magnolias
and history of lost elegance and defeat.

Nor is it the west of legend
with its great snowy peaks as backdrop
and its regal vistas of budding gold fields.

It is something better.
It is knowing
that better times are coming,
have to come.
It is promise, it is hope.
Pure and simple.

REAPING THE WIND

They came to a place where
the sky was mirrored in the land.
Vast swaths of space reaching away
to … what? Space doesn't end, does it?

They broke it with their pitiful plows
taking the guts out of the thin top loam
skimming off the cream where the grass
had held the buffalo for unbroken ages..

Now, the space is still there, but pierced
by the towering steel drills grinding away
at its underside, sucking out the black oil
and the spewing white gas, and broken, too,
by the great specters with whirling blades
reaping the wind that still sweeps the land
looking like fearful creatures imagined
by Orson Welles. But, the heart and soul
are elsewhere

CHILDREN OF THE GREAT DEPRESSION

We lived in feed sack dresses,
sometimes a flour sack.
All of us. It was no secret,
nor was it shameful.
      Except in retrospect

WILD PLUMS

Before the clouds of war gathered,
Grandfather built a clapboard house
at the edge of the Great Plains.
Grandmother painted it the color of egg yolk.
There I was born on a sunflower morning.

My father was a stubborn, silent man. Mother
was an Irish girl who danced with him until dawn,
when the west wind blew them together
and filled their pockets with dust and hope.

Father bought a team of mismatched horses
and drove us to a Saturday town. I ran behind
the wagon to prove my hardy independence
and to pick wild plums in the fence rows.

I admired socialists, hardworking anarchists,
poets, Green Corn rebels and my drunken Irish
grandfather. I married hastily and often, but rarely
repented. And never found a man who suited me.
You don't have to ask what I mean by that.

I traveled far and wide along the margins
of the mainstream, through smoky cities
and dark forests, following a narrative arc
that curved back to that rutted wagon road.

I never found a better place to take a stand
against bitterness, injustice, and all wrongs.

My life is stained by wild plums.

HOME PLACE

The little house sits on a slight rise in the surrounding plain amid the knee high prairie grasses and scrub oak we called shinnery. The weathered clapboard walls have never known paint. The gray wood has a patina almost soft to the touch. Here and there are knot holes, the knots long lost to the near constant wind.

It has only two rooms, of equal size, twelve feet by twelve feet. A small closet juts from the corner of one room, the only feature except for the sparse furnishings that distinguishes the room where we sleep from the room where we eat.

No electric wires or plumbing anchor it to the ground, yet it clings to the earth as if part of it.

On the windiest days it is indistinguishable from the powdery air. Dust sifts through the walls and around the loose fitting windows. Dust coats the dishes in the cupboard, clings to the sheets where we sleep. We breathe it in with every breath we draw in this dust bowl depression land of the 1930s.

When darkness came, we had a simple meal, sometimes nothing more than the bread my mother baked, some butter and milk from the Jersey cow my father bought at a farm auction the year he and my mother married. Afterward my father would blow out the flame burning in the kerosene lamp and we burrowed deep into our beds, the black night all about us, the wind moaning around the little house like a lonesome dog.

BLACK SUNDAY, APRIL 14, 1935

NOTE: *Stolen Memories Are Still Memories*

*What I say here may be memories I stole from Momma
because
I heard the story so many times, but if I did steal them, they
are mine now. After all, I was there and I will swear on a stack
of poems and sheet music a foot high that I clearly remember
what happened on Sunday, April 14, 1935, when I was one
year old, Momma was nineteen, Dad was twenty-one, and so
was Woody. One thing is certain: we all rode out a storm
whose fury has never been matched.*

Dawn came up white as a china teacup. A clear sky
after weeks of wind, grit, dust. Eerie, but welcome.
The sky is rainbow streaked by the time Dad hitches
his team to a walking plow, heads for the field.

Momma fires up the black wash pot in the yard of our
one-room shanty. While water heats, she gazes west
where the caprock lies, like a low cloudbank, doorstep
to the Great Plains, shining in the keen blue morning.

It's Palm Sunday, but Momma doesn't give it a thought.
We are not church-going people. We are hardworking,
Hard drinking Irish people. We go to Saturday night
house shindigs, listen to itinerant musicians play fiddles
and guitars, and dance until daylight streaks the east.

Hours later when she hangs the last pair of dungarees
on the barbwire fence, she glances west, sees a cloud
looming 10,000 feet above the plains, and shivers.

A black phantom two hundred miles wide stretching
eight hundred miles north to the Dakotas. Some said
the earth was on the move that day.

Momma grabs my blanket, her coat, and we make a run
for the nearest storm shelter a quarter mile west. At the Swope
Farm a gaggle of neighbors crowd into the earth walled cellar.
One woman, her long hair knotted on the nape of her neck,
refuses to enter the dirt shelter and begins an eerie screeching.

The wind rises and a dusty curtain drops over us.
The air turns brownish, then gray, finally a color so dark
it might be purple. A green cast defines the edge
of the clouds, thick like coarse animal hair, or steel wool.

The old woman falls to her knees facing the black
monstrosity, her hands clasped imploringly toward
the darkness, her mouth moving, but her words are torn
away by the unholy wind. The men drag the woman inside
while she begs us to get on our knees, ask the lord for mercy,
screaming, *It's the end of the world!*

The men hang on the door chain while the wind tears at it
like a fairy tale wolf, the air thick, gritty, the wind shrieking
like a banshee. My mother speak softly to the frightened
woman, quiets her. Mom wonders out loud how my father
and his horses can survive this maelstrom in an open field.

I go to sleep in Momma's lap, the storm moaning above us,
the cellar door creaking its song. She holds her hands over
my ears until the wind dies, silence comes, and we emerge
from the hole in the ground to a cold, chastened night.

We trudge home, trembling in moonless dark, find Dad
plastered with fine dust from head to toe, his plow
scattered in pieces by hysterical horses while he lies
inside a tin culvert pipe, breathing dirt.

The three of us, along with the baby boy lying serenely
in Momma's stomach, huddle together in our one bed
until another gritty day breaks.

A few miles west in Pampa, Texas, an itinerant folk singer sits
in a murky room where someone says, *This is the end of the
world*. The singer hums, *So Long, It's Been Good to Know
You*.

ODE TO DARKNESS

Before FDR's electric wires reached the pitch black prairie,
our nights were lit by kerosene lamps. As shadows turned day
to dusk, my job was to wash last night's film of soft black
soot from inside the glass globe, dried it with frayed cloth that
was once the baby's gown or a scrap of Gramp's long johns.
When the glazing was clean and clear, I poured
"coal oil" into the lamp's tank & trimmed the black wick.

There was no light on the plains save the moon and the small
holes of stars. On a cloudy night or during a new moon, the
sky went liquid black, flooding everything, the dusty road,
corrals, the scrub oak in a sea of thick heavy blackness.

We waited until murky air ate the last rags of sunlight
before we lit the readied lamp and huddled around
its flame in the middle of the kitchen table. Our hands
and faces were visible in a circle of safety around its
yellow glow that pushed shadows back into dark corners
illuminating everything that mattered in our world.

After supper we read from our dozen or so ragged books,
over and over. Mother read to aloud the laboriously penned
letters from our distant kin, Dad read haltingly week-old
editions of the Kansas City Star telling the price of beef and
pork on the hoof, cotton by the pound, in that mythical
faraway place. Mother sometimes repeated family legends,
first told by her mother, of dark times in the old south, tales of
the trek to western homesteads by landless farmers.

When the lamp sputtered on the last drops of oil, the day
ended and we went to our beds. Outside where a deep
bowl of darkness breathed the night, stars so close they
could hear us whisper, we listened to the sound of crickets,
a dog barking, the creak of a windmill turning in the wind.

COUNTRY DANCES

The Depression is all around us.
We have no place to go, nor money
to get there. Whole families cluster
on Saturday night at somebody's house.

Frank Lane and his boys make the music
picking old-time guitars, sawing away
on fiddles till daylight, stopping
only for fist fights, piss breaks
and sips from Mason jars.

Sometime after midnight I go to sleep
in the back seat of our old Plymouth.
When the cussing and fighting
break out, I awaken suddenly
wide-eyed and tense to the sound
and sight of grunting punches,
men bodies flashing and receding
in the headlights of automobiles.

My mother and other farmwomen
crowd out into the circle of light
to watch. One of them weeps.

Kids scurry around the edges, look
for the clearest view, dodge grownups.
Men stand closer, pass bottles,
or wade into it, like my father does.

Sweating farm boys and men crouch
or lunge at each other, get knocked
to the ground, get up again, wipe blood

smears on torn shirts, eyes dart here, there,
trying to focus, kicking up puffs of dust
in yellow air cast by incandescent headlights.

It ends, the loser down in the dirt,
his eyes glazed, someone stands
above him, waiting, wheezing.
Women sigh and exhale.

I see it over and over, summer dance
after summer dance, until the bright day
I was free to leave that despised place,
that place to which I am bound
by an unbreakable thread that expands
to every point in the known universe.

WHERE HOME IS

There is a place I have called home all of my life,
a place where I am always present even when I am
somewhere else. A place that is part of me, a place
where I am always leaving, always returning.

I am in love with the history of that place, its agrarian values
of another era, my family's role in that.
Its impact on my life. I mourn the losses and would regain
what has been lost if I could.

Some say, home is where the heart is,
Others say, home is where the wealth is.
Though I doubt either is totally true,
I think romanticism is closer than wealth
in finding one's home.

One thing I know for sure is that we all
want a place to call home. Another thing
I know for certain is that when I found my true self,
my other self, my soul mate, I found where home is.

2.
GENEALOGY

LABOR OMNIA VINCIT

"Both gods and men are angry with a man who lives idle,
for in nature he is like the stingless drones who waste
the labour of the bees, eating without working."
Hesiod, *Works and Days (II. 293-319)*

The influences of my childhood, my father, my mother, my paternal grandmother, their words, the examples they set, tattooed the value of work on my psyche, my mind and my heart.

They taught that tilling dirt was near sacred. Nay, that it was indeed sacred. To stir the soil was our sacred duty. To wield a plow, a rake, your foot, or whatever object was within reach.

To breed and nurture the animals that gave us meat and milk, to find the wild ones who could serve our needs. To labor on throughout the day and into the night if necessary. That regardless of however you might transgress otherwise, there was always salvation and forgiveness in hard work. It was the closest thing we had to a religion

Some believe that life begins when the chores are done.
Our family believes that doing the chores *is* life.

CULTIVATING COMFORT

My grandmother sought solace in dirt. Digging, planting, hoeing, raking in her garden. I remember cutting the seed potatoes in chunks leaving only enough potato around each eye to nourish the birth of a new vine. Because we were Irish or because we were superstitious, or because we were both, we rose at the crack of dawn on St. Patrick's day to plant the dried chunks in a furrow she gouged out with a hoe in the half frozen sod. We dropped the eyes into the furrow at precise intervals, covered them with dirt and tamped them down with our wet, mud caked shoes.

Having satisfied St. Patrick and grandmother, we were allowed the warmth of her kitchen and a farm breakfast. For the occasion she saved the last of the bacon from the winter butchering, mostly white greasy fat saturated with salt. She boiled it, then dipped it in flour and fried it crisp. This, along with her soft fried eggs and biscuits the size of softballs almost compensated for the cold morning of work.
For weeks we watched the garden for crust broken by the first furled leaf born from chilly ground. Daily we checked to see the progress rising green into the spring air. When she decreed the time right, we dug up vines, sifted spuds from the dirt and stored them in the musty cellar outside her kitchen door. In celebration she boiled a pot full in their tender peels.

I confess that the taste of new potatoes with butter, salt and pepper has its own rewards, but it never inspired me to become a dirt farmer. I miss none of the chores of digging and planting and harvesting.

Still, I do remember the comfort it brought to the dear old woman and now I, too, forage for the same relief among scraps of written words, trying to make them bear fruit before the worms in this weary garden take me under.

PLANTING BEANS IN THE DUST BOWL

for my grandmother, Delure Elizabeth Holbrook Yowell

She bends straight over, no squatting for her,
makes hills with her hoe, drops the beans in the hill.
She walks the rows without stopping, shooing away
grasshoppers, until all the hills have three bean seeds
snuggled in like babies in a feather bed. Then she goes
to the well, fills her ten-quart bucket, tips a cupful
on each hill, all the water those beans will see for a month.

Though hard to see how it happens, she harvests
basket after basket of beans in the fall and puts them up
feeds her family through the long howling winter.

Whatever her secret it worked for everything she did.

HITCH HIKING TO HEAVEN

When I was a small girl, about eight or nine years old, my father took the family on a Sunday outing to a ranch rodeo, a "ropin" as everybody called them. We drove to a working ranch near the town of Canadian in the Texas panhandle.

It was a country sort of thing. My mother took a basket of food: fried chicken (which taunted us with its smell all the way there), biscuits, new potatoes boiled whole in their red skins, and fried okra. We also brought a gallon jug of water, which we drank the first hour there. But, not to worry. There was a water well with a windmill near the cattle pens, and we refilled our jug — twice.

It was a fine day; we had lots of fun, my little sister and brother and me. We play on the corral fences, in the mud around the water tank, and even watched the bucking broncs, bull riders, and the calf roping --- not to mention the funny clown whose antics distracted the snorting bulls away from their tormentors after they had dumped the spurred cowboys on the ground.

It was dusk by the time we left and the three of us slept all the way home, curled up with each other, our mouths open, in the back seat of Dad's old '35 Plymouth.

Unhappily, the euphoria was short-lived. The next day we were in misery. We had big stomach aches, retching, vomiting, fever and chills. Even Mom and Dad were sick.

Old Doc Cary showed about noon. I'll never know how he heard we were sick because we certainly didn't have a telephone in those days. Nevertheless, he came in through front door swearing like a sailor as usual, examined all of us, asked a few terse questions, especially about what and where we had eaten and where we drank water. He then announced that we had typhoid fever. (Later he determined it came from that well at the rodeo pens.)

Because typhoid was highly contagious and patients required expert care, he said he would get word to my grandmother who lived in the village of Reydon, our Saturday town.

To this day, I don't know how she got there so quickly, but she showed up before dark that same day, walking. She carried a large bundle of home remedies, worn out sheets and pillow cases, along with some groceries.

My grandmother did not drive, nor did my grandfather. They didn't even own a car. She relied on her four sons to provide transportation for them when it was needed, which wasn't often because they lived within walking distance of the grocery store and all the other places they needed to go. But World War II was going on and two sons were away fighting the war, a third one was at work and couldn't be reached, and, of course, my father was in no fit state to go get her. So, she walked miles carrying all that stuff in large bundles.

She was in her late fifties at the time and was used to walking great distances — and working hard. She milking cows twice a day, planted a large vegetable garden, tended a fruit orchard, and did most of the farming, since my grandfather had suffered a stroke in his late forties and was paralyzed on his left side. She could harness and drive a team of horses, but preferred traveling on foot. Although she would accept a ride if she knew the driver or if he or she looked reliable.

She stayed with us for two weeks, nursing all five of us through the ravages of typhoid fever. She made fresh meat broth for us every day because that's all we could eat. She washed our bed linens every day . . . by hand. There was no washing machine because there was no electricity.

She also disposed of our bodily fluids by burying them a half mile downstream from our well to keep the bacteria from migrating into the water supply.

When we were well enough to look after ourselves, she packed up her gear and set out on foot for home.

This was not an unusual thing for her to do. She was the hardiest good Samaritan I have ever seen before or since she left this earth.

After I became old enough to have a driver's license, she asked me to teach her how to drive an automobile and I promised her I would. However, to my great shame and regret, I never got around to it. I am haunted by my failure to do that one thing that she wanted so much.

She believed in heaven and if there is such a place, she was certainly entitled to go . . . even if she had to walk to get there.

DISCIPLINARIAN

My first memory of him:
I smell rain coming across
the field and see my father,
still young, running toward us,
drops of rain peppering his shirt,
like tiny lights
flashing in darkness.

Brawny and fearless,
he can swim under water
without getting it in his nose.
He stands between us
and the things
that would hurt us.
With him we are safe
from the world.

But who is there
to keep us safe from him.

GOOD TIMES

Bologna on white bread
with faux mayonnaise
— that cheap salad dressing —
and a dozen NeHi orange soda pops.

A feast, in the back of his Chevy pickup
hooked to a stinking trailer
knee deep in cow dung
parked in shade behind the auction barn
where farmers gathered on Thursdays
to bid and yell, buy and sell.

Back at home Mother interrogated
and chastised us, knowing full well
what had gone on when she saw
the joy in her children's eyes
and the stains on our dirty faces.

THE LAST ROOSEVELT, APRIL 12, 1945

A sunny, blustery day, the wind raising sand, stinging my skinny legs as I step down from the old school bus, a rickety affair, wooden benches, no heat in winter, leaky roof. The first thing I see is the smoldering carcass of our old Ford in the earth-packed side yard, burned out hulk, no seats, no window glass. I am sad and scared. Inside the house, my mother is crying, my father somber. Tears verging in my own eyes. I say, *Can't we get another car?* Teary-eyed, Mother says, *we don't care about the car. President Roosevelt is dead.*

My father makes a small sound and bolts from the house. He doesn't want anyone to see him cry.

I am left wondering where we will find another Roosevelt because Franklin D. had been president all of my life, and I thought Roosevelt meant "president."

BOXING LESSONS

My father was a boxer, addicted to fist fighting. He wanted to pass this trait to a genetic heir. I was not the best candidate. But, I was the only one available at the time he had the idea.

He laced his gloves on me, so big the cuffs reached my elbows. So heavy it was a chore for me to merely lift them, a gargantuan effort to punch someone. *No excuses,* he would say.

Get your dukes up like I showed you. One hand guards your face, the other one guards your stomach, the places you don't want to get hit.

Now, dance on your toes, keep moving. One glove up as a shield, the other jabbing your opponent.

My opponent?! For God's sake, it was Loretta, the neighbor girl, two years older, a head taller.arms two inches longer than mine, she laughed as she held me at arm's length with one hand, punched me in the face with the other one. She bloodied my nose, time after time, while I flailedaway in midair. Never touching her one time. For her it was a lark. She always won.

Disgusted with my poor showing, my father finally released me from the tortured 'lessons.' I went back to my books, my incessant scribbling.

He considered me an abject failure until years later when he noticed striking similarities between the practice of law and fist fighting.

MASTER OF THE SOIL

My father bends to the ground, palms a dob of dirt, touches
it to his tongue like a French chef testing his soup du jour.

At sixteen years, he has a vision, sees himself owning land,
ploughing, growing cotton, broomcorn, alfalfa, maize, wheat.
He sees fields, fallow under his walking plow, grass and grain
billowing in the Oklahoma wind like waves on an open sea,
this prairie he knows so well. His hands feel the long leather
lines stretching from the horses' collars, plow handles, worn
silky smooth and gray, polished by sweat from his fingers, the
steel plow slicing through the prairie sod, opening a track that
a million buffalo have trod up and down these ancient plains,
galloping through the eons.

He shapes this dream with his bare hands, a team of good
horses, a young wife whose labor is equal to his own and
more, but riches elude those who scratch the surface of this
gritty ground. The wind lifts their toil into the vault of blue,
carries it away. He grows old, he wearies, sees his sons, and
their sons caught in the swirling cloud of never coming rest,
subsistence always an inch beyond their grasp.

His back is weak, his will is firm as he signs the papers
they bring to him. He lives to see the steel augers harvest
the elusive wealth from the depths of his longing, lives to see
fields desecrated, furrows, fences, terraces torn asunder,
creeks of black oily waste, money in the bank.

He dies wondering if the price was too high.

DEBTS OWED MY FATHER

My father, when resentful of something
I said or did, reminded me that I owed him
for my "upbringing." He roughly estimated
the dollars expended, as well as the loss
of the wonderful life he might have lived
had he not been "saddled" with a wife
and a gaggle of ungrateful children.

To my credit, I suppose, he did in later years
tell me I was the only one of his children
who came close to repaying their debt to him.
Curiously, he never calculated Mother's share,
or, for that matter, ever stated whether or not
we owed her anything at all.

THE END OF WILDNESS

Let me tell you how much my father was part of the land,
and the wild places on this earth. When young he lived
among the wild things, great and small: carp, catfish,
flatheads, channel cat, perch, skunks, muskrats, coyotes,
beaver, rabbit, wild and not wild, creatures of his heart.

How he loved them, and lived by rules of their kingdom,
survival of the fittest, tilting for the upper hand, blood
the prize. How they fought to save themselves from him,
his blood mingling with theirs in the rivers, creeks
and sloughs of plains and near plains. How he brought
their young home to meet us, and we learned their ways,
loved them and saw them return to the wilderness
when it the time came. How narrow are the places left
for men like my father to be one with the wilderness.

RIGHTEOUS ANGER

Melancholy drifted around my mother
like dry leaves from the mimosa tree
in her yard when her son, nineteen years old,
left to fight a distant war, at the whim of old men
wreathed in cigar smoke and dreams of power.
Sitting in buttery leather chairs far removed
from the blood and bullets, they played with young lives
as if they were Chinese checkers or poker chips.

She saw the divide, the abyss, the distance between
promise and fact, and yearned to close the breach.
She was angry and heart broken, felt helpless.
In despair, she challenged her husband, the nearest
patriarch and symbol of power within her reach.

To that end, she declared her independence
from marriage as she has always known it.
She stood her ground, defied my father.
Set herself free. Like Sojourner Truth

MY MOTHER'S EDUCATION

October, 1968, a Friday night.

.

A few dozen people, including me, sit in folding chairs in a small auditorium at a Vocational Technical School in the miniscule town of Burns Flat, Oklahoma. We are here to see members of our families receive certificates denoting completion of training courses. It's a rather motley crew --- I count twenty-six graduates --- mostly girls and women trained as nurses' aides or licensed practical nurses, and a few gangly young men in clean but permanently oil stained coveralls who will become mechanics, most likely repairing farm machinery and trucks in the farming communities of western Oklahoma.

All are recognizable as products of this dry, wind-swept countryside. Dust Bowl survivors and their descendants, people who work with their hands and do the best they can under harsh conditions.

The audience is obviously of the same demographic, except they are a generation older than those who rise to receive the rolled certificates tied with blue ribbons. Except for me. I have driven here from Oklahoma City to see my fifty-four-year-old mother (the most senior of the students) rewarded for more than a year of hard work under near impossible circumstances. She has come here five days a week for fourteen months, driving her old second-hand car eighty miles each way each day. She has labored long and hard to decipher the printed course materials with her seventh grade education she abandoned forty years ago to work in her father's fields.

She has endured the wrath of my father who has berated her daily for doing this.

She has surmounted the stumbling blocks he placed in her path. She has accomplished her goal: she is now a certified dietetic technician. This means she is qualified to plan and prepare meals
for persons confined to health care facilities, like nursing homes and hospitals. It means she is employable. Someone will pay her money for her work. She has a piece of paper attesting to the fact. She has value. She is her own person.

I am her witness.

As we drive home, we see an Indian powwow in progress on the outskirts of Elk City. Dancing figures cast wild shadows as they circle round a fire. My mother says, "Oh, let's stop and watch. I need to see this."

The night is cool but not uncomfortable; it is pleasant to listen to the drums and singing of the Cheyenne and Arapaho peoples. The Head Dancer announces an "inter-tribal" dance which means that non-native people in the audience may participate. My mother and I, with only a knowing glance between us, wordlessly join the Indian women and dance a circuit around the fire.

MY MOTHER BITES THE BIG APPLE

Without doubt, my mother was a countrywoman, born in the San Bois Mountains of eastern Oklahoma, and reared in rural areas of this state. She met my father when her family of migrant farm workers came west during cotton harvest. They stayed on for a couple of years, but during the dustbowl-depression years, her family moved back to the east side. She stayed and married my father. They lived there on a farm for the rest of their lives.

She was not a world traveler. She had hardly set foot outside the boundaries of Oklahoma until her grown children began taking her on road trips. She was game for these forays, but always with that inborn country-bred suspicion of strangers and strange places.

Nor was she an air traveler. She had never seen the inside of a commercial plane until the spring of 1973 when she somewhat reluctantly agreed to get on one bound for New York City. It was to visit her oldest grandchild, Kim Alexander, in the U.S. Navy stationed on Long Island. She was anxious but excited as she made plans on what to wear and the places she wanted to visit. She confided to us that she had always wanted to see Macy's Department Store and Jack Dempsey's restaurant in Manhattan. We had no idea that she harbored such ambitions as she went about her life as a farmer's wife in rural Oklahoma. (We didn't even know Jack Dempsey had a restaurant in New York City.)

The day before we left, my brother Clark, took a $100 bill from his wallet and said, "Here, Mom, buy something at Macy's for yourself, or a drink at Jack Dempsey's." She took it as a sign that the trip would be a good one.

Surprisingly, she appeared at ease on the flight from Oklahoma City to Chicago, eager to see what the country looked like from thousands of feet up, amazed at how it the plane was traveling over 300 miles per hour but seemed to be standing still, and at the novelty of the foods served by the chic stewardesses. She laughed as she looked down on the Chicago downtown loop, crowds of people the likes of which she had never seen in her life.

She showed no anxiety as our plane circled the Big Apple for almost 20 minutes waiting for a landing space. She was curious but subdued in the huge crush of people and the noise of LaGuardia Airport as we collected our bags and found a taxicab to take us to Long Island. She did lecture the cabdriver, a young Italian immigrant who kept turning around to talk a steady stream to us as we careened through the streets and tunnels. She said twice, "Young man, keep your eyes on the road, please."

As we made our way around the city, as different as it could be from her little country village, I gained a new respect for my mother's poise and ability to adjust and to enjoy herself in these strange surroundings. I decided that she was far more sophisti-cated than I had suspected.

The day came to go shopping at Macy's. The place was almost a city in itself. We spent a considerable amount of time examining the merchandise, testing fabrics between thumb and forefinger, looking at labels, checking prices. She finally selected a very colorful, expensive silk scarf and made her way to the cashier. When the cost was rung up, the scarf placed in its fancy little bag, and it was time to pay, Mom said, "Excuse me," turned slightly away from the clerk and reached into the top of her dress. Then, to my horror, I saw a huge safety pin anchoring the $100 dollar bill to her brassiere. She swiftly unpinned the bill, tucked her undergarment back inside her dress and nonchalantly handed the money to the clerk.

The clerk never betrayed any surprise at this, behaving as if everyone carried their money in their underwear. Mother never missed a lick either. I was the only one with a red face.

PATRIARCH
for my father, Earnest Yowell

A white room, white sheets,
in white silence, he lies like a block
of granite, as gray and weathered
as the clapboards of the old house
where they lived before the war.

His solid stillness is betrayed
only by the machine, bubbling
and humming, its needles scratching
ragged lines on a spooled graph.

While his strength drains into the space
around the bed, his children stand, like
nervous sentinels half expecting
the stone to roll away from the tomb,
waiting, waiting, breathing shallow
breaths without sound.

And in the whiteness, the boatman
waits for his passenger to board,
to leave his iron habits behind,
his stiff opinions, dry and hard
as old crockery, chipped and cracked.

All wait and wait,
for the old man to say when.

I ASK MY FATHER TO SING

At the Senior Living Center,
I ask my father to sing.
He sits up straight like a school boy
and begins an old Jimmie Rodgers tune,
Just Waitin' for a Train

Now, I've never been a thousand miles
from home without a penny to my name,
never been kicked off a train in Texas,
nor slept out in the rain. But I love to hear
him sing it in his quavering old voice.

When he sees my tears,
he reaches for his harmonica
And says, "Let's have something
cheerful, let's do a jig."

If my mother were still alive,
she would smile and say,
He never could carry a tune.

ELEGY FOR PARENTS

A thread runs through millennia of chromosomes,
through prairie grasses blown about by winds
of rage, shared blood, hard work, longing,
sadness, and triumph. A thread as steely
as the lines used to catch wild game fish, those
with rows of angry teeth fighting to their death.

As much as I rebelled against them and their opposite
 ways, I see my own image in the same mirror. I turn
away, and feel their eyes follow me like a perceptual
painting. I see their shadows converge with the one
I cast on that rough ground between the trails we follow
to other worlds, separate but eternally bound.

FAMILY REUNION

We're all here where the chairs are arranged
so everyone is face to face with everyone else.
It's the only time we see each other all at once.

In this room waiting while another member
of this family fades from the circle, old grudges
are put aside, feuds are given up for the day.
Time enough to resume, after the wake, after
the camaraderie is forgotten, the polite exchanges
dying into silence. Even affectionate connections
will veer off to separate lines barely remembering
how we came together in a rush of shared genes
and gestures, likenesses outweighing differences,
remembering the old ones who once held us
together when we were all someone else. Before
we unlinked and reinvented ourselves as strangers,
to prove we were different, to show we could
do better, rise above the common thread.

But when one of us is threatened with annihilation,
being cut down, the elastic strand contracts
pulling us in tight, if only for a moment,
before we expand again into our separate worlds

WHEN WE WERE HORSES
For Cecil, 1936-1947

Straddling carefully chosen cane stalks
or, better still, a sturdy broom handle,
we urged ourselves on with switches,
pawing the ground, whinnying,
nostrils flaring, eyes rolled back
in wild horseness.

Hooves ringing on the dry earth,
we raced over the prairie as free
as the west wind bending grasses
low, manes flying behind us
like flags in a breeze.

We did not know the word "cancer" then,
did not know it could take down
a horse and rider, or a ten-year-old
prancing centaur.

(My younger brother died when he was ten years old. I was twelve.
My sister, Mary, was only seven, and my brother, Clark, was a babe
of two months. Cecil had been sick for almost two years before he
died.)

A HERO REMEMBERED

In memory of my Uncle Tony Yowell who served in the 45th Division, 179th Infantry, was captured at the battle for Anzio Beachhead, Italy, January 1944 and was a POW at Stalag III-B until the camp was liberated by the Soviets

He carried me on his shoulders
when July sand burned my bare feet,
bought bags of licorice ropes
to soothe the pain of sulking

Broke my heart when
he left a soft life
in my grandmother's house
to cowboy on the Gunnison in '38

He hitchhiked back to Oklahoma
through a Christmas blizzard carrying
a two-foot doll in cellophane
that I named Molly

In '42 he left us all crying at the depot
and marched off with Patton
and the 45th Division to North Africa
Sicily and Anzio

In 1944 he sent a Postkart marked
Stalag III-B saying
take care of grandma and grandpa

There was a parade when he came home
After that he married the grass widow
down the road and broke my heart again

TRAVELING THE MILKY WAY
for Kim Alexander, 1953-1989

On nights like this when he drifts through
her dreams like smoke from burning wood,
it helps to rise, to step out into darkness,
hear coyotes howling on the western ridge,
the moon skulking behind the gnarled elms,
stars hovering so close they can hear her breathe.

She imagines his bitter sweet presence.
Not on this planet where she is stranded
but out there among the receding points
in the realm of Orion and his heavy belt
a million million light years away.

She whispers his name and waits, like the nights
of his boyhood, when aflame with need to share
the wonders of the night sky, he whispered her awake,
showed her distant worlds through his telescope.

She imagines him now as one of those ancient
lights, in a heaven of his own choosing.

*My beloved son, Kim Alexander, succumbed to the ravages
of HIV/AIDS in 1989, just 80 days after the disease was
diagnosed. His death is, and shall remain, the greatest
watershed of my life. Because of him, I was able to find a new
way to live. I am grateful for his short existence on this earth
and for his great selfless generosity.*

ROCK GARDEN

for Kim Alexander, 1953-1989

Each one is smooth, round, Zen like,
polished by waves of a thousand seas.

Each one gathered by a boy whose wiry
body I still see bent like a question mark
over tide pools on the Bay of Fundy,
the oily Gulf Coast, sands of the Outer Banks,
a river running swift in a mile deep canyon,
and along all the roads he ever traveled.

Each one rests here in my garden now,
reminding me that nothing lives long
but the earth
                  and the stones.

WHAT REMAINS: Elegy
For My Son

I quit believing in heaven years ago,
but I yearn for some kind of illusion.
One where I *know* his presence again.
Something solid and sensory

like the smell of his shirts in the closet
after he was gone. The ones I buried
my face in when the tide of sadness
washed over me in the tired hours.

I would be consoled to see his face
once more – even for a moment –
as in a flash of lightning, and to kiss
his soft cheek one last time before I die.

They say the last moments of dying
are like falling in love. I hope that's
so, because I fell in love the day
he was born and never got over it.

LAMENT

For my nephew, Eric Randall Erickson, 1960 – 2011
the boy who sprung from the ground on the Texas plains

What say the waves,
the water,
the wind,
the loons?

Do they know sorrow?
Do they know how
the earth split open,
and swallowed up the joy?

Does the eagle know who was taken?
Do the animals of the woods mourn?

What can be said
of wildness
of a boat racing into the gale,
a roaring cycle
tearing the sunlight asunder,

now that the unthinkable
has happened? Now that
earth and sky have opened
and loosed the sorrow.

Ashes blow over the ice,
our hearts find no place
to warm their hands.

The land is frozen and barren,
We will wait for light and warmth
not knowing when it will return.

A MAN WITH NO ENEMIES
for Jeff Yowell, 1951-2015

Somberly we file into the silent
room where he lies flat, still, rigid.
My first thought is to find a blanket.
He looks cold, I expect him to shiver.

His son cups a hand over his graying
head and weeps, my breath catches sharply
in my chest like swallowing a stone.
The unthinkable has caught us unaware.

I still remember the night he was born,
the house ablaze with light, all of us there
waiting for him. His mother, his father,
the gruff old country doctor.

A red haired child with a timid smile;
a man of uncommon strength & goodness,
who, last night, without a word, stepped
out alone & unafraid into the darkness.

*My brother, Jeff, was a gentle man, yet strong and stalwart. I took
the title for this poem from a comment by a news reporter in our tiny
hometown newspaper who described him that way, a man with no
enemies. Almost the entire community turned out for his memorial
service, even though he was a liberal Democrat in a blood-red
community where hardly anybody was of like mind. He never
backed down from his deeply held personal beliefs. He was true to
his principles.*

TRIP TO WYUKA

for Paul Brandhorst, 1966-1998

His first night at support group he wore
a western hat low over his eyes, a toothpick
 in the side of his mouth, thumbs hooked
 in Levi pockets, pretended to be a cowboy.

He said nothing save his name but afterwards
followed me out to ask a question, the kind you
just know is an excuse for conversation. I had seen
enough before this night to know how it would go.

His family had scattered like quail
at the mention of AIDS, were still in hiding.
He was driven by the unfairness, injustice,
bitterness, loneliness. Under the brim
of the Stetson he was desperate to connect.

Near the end he asked to see his mother's grave
in Nebraska. We walked the streets of Lincoln,
while he pointed out landmarks, his mother's
grave in Wyuka Cemetery, the pauper's plot
of infamous Charlie Starkweather.

Our second time in Lincoln, I carried him
in an urn, left him in that place where mothers,
sons and murderers lie down together, all injustice
and bitterness swallowed up in the dirt.

*Paul Brandhorst was a young man who came to live in my home for
a time after his family abandoned him when they found he had
HIV/AIDS. He was a sweet, shy man with little education, but with a
good heart. Like a "son" to me after I lost my own child. (This poem
was awarded the 2013 Christopher Hewitt Poetry Prize and
appeared in the August 2013 Issue of A&U Magazine.)*

3.
IN MEDIA RES

HOW WORLD WAR II BEGAN

Early one Sunday morning in December the year I turned seven years old, Dad went to feed his cattle and noticed a hole in the corral fence and some of the cattle were missing. Their tracks lead toward the west on the unpaved highway running by our house. They would be easy to follow tracks in the sandy roadbed. Dad saddled old Nancy, our gentle mare, told Momma not to wait breakfast for him because he didn't know how long he would be gone.

We ate breakfast without him, and even waited a long time before we ate at noon, again without him. Mama was anxious, worried that he had met with an accident. Finally, at almost dark, he came home driving the truant cattle. His face had a stern expression, his mood was solemn. When Mama began to chastise him about his lateness, he stopped her by saying, "I have been listening to the radio at Swope's house. The Japs have bombed Pearl!"

Of course, he said a lot of other things, too, but all I could think about was that Japs had dropped bombs on "Pearl." Of all people, why had they chosen "Pearl?" The only Pearl I knew was an elderly neighbor by that name, a terrible gossip who Momma had cautioned us about. Pearl would approach kids when their parents weren't near and ask questions about family personal business. So, we were careful to avoid Pearl whenever we saw her coming. So, I was very alarmed when it sounded to me like the Japs and had flown their airplanes to Oklahoma and dropped bombs on an old farm lady. Even if she repeated gossip about someone, it seemed harsh to my seven-year-old self that she would be blown up.

And, who would they pick to bomb next? It seemed to me it could be anybody since they were obviously in the neighbor-hood. At that prospect, I began to cry uncontrollably.

Momma could hardly keep a straight face when she explained that the bombs had fallen on a *place* named Pearl Harbor far, far away in Hawaii. I wasn't thoroughly convinced that we were safe from the villainous Japs, and for months I still listened intently when I heard an airplane and looked for hiding places just in case the bombs started falling.

BEFORE DR. SPOCK

Before I learned to read I learned to work.
Before the sun rose over the sloping barn roof
Before the horses were hayed and harnessed

I learned to fill water jugs, load the wheelbarrow
to park it in the shade and to wait for the call
of thirsty men and thirsty horses to summon me

As the sun rose, as heat pelted the laden fields
I heaved the barrow down the rows and imagined
myself one of those Saint Bernard dogs saving lives
in deep Alpine snow high upon cloud piercing peaks

earning no gold or riches, other than the nod
of approval from the patriarch, my father

FIRST LOVE

for Charles S., wounded for life in Korea, 1952

A green breeze blows softly from the south,
mellow and sensuous, the consistency
of melting ice cream, smoothing out wrinkles,
as we lie outside on a hard cotton mattress
still warm from the sun. Giant stars float
in their deep blue-black bowl. Melancholy that
comes at end of day, holds us in perfect tension.
I am convinced we have invented a new emotion,
the first to know this burning thing between us.
I want to remember this night until the day I die.

EARLY AMBITIONS

Back then, I wanted to channel Silvia Beach,
run away to Paris, open a bookstore,
a lending library, get to know Hemingway,
James Joyce, Scott Fitzgerald. I wanted to meet
Alice B. Toklas, lure her away from Gertrude
Stein and live with her on the West Bank,
strolling through sidewalk cafes, translating
the Iliad, baking her brownies, making jokes,
gossiping, living the Bohemian life .

But my father would never allow such a thing.
And my mother would have called it ungrateful.

LETTER TO MY SISTER
for Mary Yowell Erickson

You were the athlete, right from the beginning.
I should never have tried to compete, signing up
for that junior varsity team, trying to be a jock.
I was not cut from such cloth. Not basketball material.

In those days girls played half court, six players:
three guards, three forwards. Only the forwards
could shoot, make baskets, get the roar of applause
from bleachered parents, whistles, stamping feet, glory.

They made me a guard. Guards were drones,
their job was to interfere, get the ball, stop others
from dropping the ball through the hoop,
get stepped on, get cursed, get penalized for fouls.

Negative efforts rewarded. Didn't work for me.
First play, I got my hands on the ball. I ran. I dribbled.
I pivoted. I threw the ball. It sailed high overhead
in a perfect arc, like a Roman candle throwing sparks.

I watched it falling in slow motion above the basket
saw it drop with a whisper into the net, dead center,
not touching the rim. My heart on fire followed it.
TWO POINTS! Ecstasy. The crowd rose, roared.

My heart soared. The moment of truth was mine.
But, wait. Ashes and dust. Shame and disgrace.
The points counted for the other side. Red face.

Coda: Thankfully, your graceful leaps, bounds
        and rebounds, whisper of ball through the net
        erased the stain of my pathetic faux pas!

DISOBEDIENCE

It was a point of honor not to do what she told us to do
when she left us alone, my sister and me. Not right away.
We'd do a lot of other stuff first, play a few of her old, heavy,
scratchy Victrola records, play a couple of hands of Old
Maid, go outside and kick some rocks, anything but what she
told us to do.

When it was dangerously close to time for her return, we
frantically ran the hot water, dumped in soap granules,
gathered the plates with congealed gravy, the silverware with
crusted egg yolk, coffee-stained cups. We crazily crammed
them into the enameled dishpan. When the sound
of her Ford coming up the lane reached us, we assumed
expressions of oppressed peoples, grabbed the dishrag, the
drying cloth, and waited for her moans of exasperation,
hoping she would not resort to the wooden spoon the used as a
paddle.

THE CHRONICLES OF CAMILLA

or

Everything I Know About Life I Learned From My College Roommate

1.

Her name was Camilla, the youngest of twelve children born to Lebanese immigrant parents. She was absolutely outrageous. She was two years older than me and I was in love with her.

It was 1952 and I was green as a gourd when I came to the little community college only 40 miles from the farm where I grew up. It might as well have been on the other side of the moon.

I was as gullible as one can get, and she saw me coming. She recognized me as grist for her flim-flam mill.

The second week of classes, I got an after-school job at the Rexall Drug where she worked.

I was hired to work the soda fountain, a soda jerk.

Camilla immediately established the pecking order by informing me that her title was "sales clerk," presumably a position above mine.

The owner, Mrs. Randall, a trim dignified 60-something woman, tended to shake her head and roll her eyes at Camilla's goofy statements, as if to say, "you two work out your relationship problems and leave me out of it."

2.

I was no match for Camilla. She was the most exotic creature I had ever met and I thought she knew a whole lot of things I needed to know if I was to become a woman of the world. My most ardent ambition.

I thought that's what she was! A woman of the world!

She immediately took charge of me. Literally. She insisted that I move out of my rented room and into her apartment. And share the rent, of course. The way she explained it made perfect sense to me, so I did.

She wasn't mean or vicious, but she did have control issues. She messed with my head. Just because she could. Or, because it amused her. She seemed to enjoy it when I swallowed one of her goofy declarations.

I've decided she was part 8th grade boy!

3.

She declared me a "hick" and undertook to "educate" me. She began by teaching me the language she and her family spoke in their home. She said her name meant "finish" in Lebanese. Said her father gave her the name because twelve children were enough and he declared she would be the last one. That sounded reasonable to me, and I was happy to think I had learned my first Lebanese word.

She also taught me other phrases that she suggested I use in speaking to Mr. Albert, the old Lebanese man who delivered our huge cartons of ice cream. So, I would cheerfully greet him with the words she taught me, sounding something like "shehebic ana iwan ente." I always thought the shocked looks he gave me were because of my bad pronunciation. Years later the same friend informed me that I was greeting poor old Mr. Albert with something like, "may you grow like an onion with your head in the dirt!"

4.

The drugstore was in an old fashioned building on the corner of Main and 4th Street. Fourth Street was U.S. Route 66, the Mother Road.

In 1952 Eisenhower had not yet built Interstate Highway 40, so we sat on the main thoroughfare through the middle of the America. We looked out through large plate glass windows and watched America passing by. And America looked back at us.

In the front corner window area, with the most natural light, Arthur Logan, the watch repairman and jeweler, sat. He rented

the space from Mrs. Randall, and he had a vantage point. He could see all the travelers coming and going in four directions, as well as each customer who entered or left the store. He also had a clear view of everything we did behind the soda fountain.

Arthur was fussy. He had a mousy submissive wife and he preferred all women be that way. I'm sure he was frustrated to have Mrs. Randall as his landlord and overseer, but there was nothing he could do about that. So, he concentrated on trying to bring Camilla and me to heel. He didn't make much headway because Camilla thwarted him at every turn, so he became a tattle tale.

There was one thing that annoyed him more than anything else. We blended shakes and malts in stainless steel canisters.

Usually there was a bit left over after we filled the fancy malt glasses we served the customers in. Rather than throw it away,

Camilla and I drank it. If Mrs. Randall, or Kenneth the pharmacist was watching, we poured it into a small glass before drinking it, but if not, we drank it from the canister. This annoyed Arthur beyond his ability to control himself.

First, he tried yelling at us, but when we ignored him and continued our disgusting habit, he snitched to Mrs. Randall. She quietly told us to stop, and added the caveat that it "upset" Arthur. I got the impression that Mrs. R. also thought he was a jerk, though she never actually said that.

Once when he complained to her in our presence, Mrs. R turned to us, and said, "If you girls don't stop that, I am going to send you to Malt Canister Drinkers Anonymous." We laughed, and, of course, it only further infuriated Arthur.

Finally, Camilla devised a way to get revenge on Arthur. When repairing a watch, he took the tiny pieces off one by one and laid them separately on a small square of cloth and placed a clear glass bowl upside down over the pieces. Thus, he kept from scattering the pieces and prevented dust from collecting on the mechanism.

But, he also worked on more than one at a time. I don't know why. Maybe it was necessary to order replacement parts and wait for them to arrive. At any rate, he sometimes had as many as three or four separate repair jobs going at one time on his work counter, which itself was glass covered.

Therein lay the seeds of Camilla's revenge. When he left the store for lunch or went home before we did, and when no one was looking and she went behind Arthur's counter and mixed a few parts from one watch with another. Not a wholesale mix, but enough.

It drove Arthur crazy sometimes, trying to make the parts work. We all, including Camilla and me, commiserated with him on how the little parts stubbornly refused to go back where they obviously came from.

He fussed. He swore. He almost sobbed at times! He complained, he ruminated. But, for some unknown reason, he never seemed to suspect that someone was deliberately mixing up the parts!

5.

Camilla not only supervised my work at the Rexall Drug, but she set the pace in the cramped little apartment where we lived. She made the grocery lists, she decided what we ate, and how it was cooked. That part was fine with me because she brought a lot of food that her Lebanese mother had made for us. Kebbeh, cabbage rolls, tabbouleh, hummus. The beginning of life-long affinity for Mediterranean food for me.

She also directed my personal habits. Every morning when we awoke, she had a combination beauty and health routine for us to do. We raised our arms to should height, bent our elbows, put our fists together and began a backward and forward motion of our arms, chanting with each move, "I must, I must increase my bust."

The exercise worked better for her than it did for me.

6.

One of our duties at the drugstore was to wrap the boxes of
sanitary napkins and tampons in plain wrapping paper and tie
the package with twine string, so nobody could tell what you
had bought. That's how it was in the 1950s. Menstrual periods
were sometimes referred to as "the sick time of month."

The first time it was my turn to wrap the Kotex boxes, she
went to the greeting card rack and selected a dozen "get well"
cards and told me to put one inside the wrapping on each box,
as a gesture of good will. She thought it would be help get
more business. It showed that Rexall Drug cared.

Sounded like a brilliant idea to me, so I dutifully place a card
in each wrapped box . . . Until Mrs. Randall saw me doing it,
and said, "where did you get such a ridiculous idea? Stop it
right now."

I was disappointed in Mrs. Randall for not seeing what a great
public relations move it was.

7.

One slow Sunday afternoon I saw her sitting on the front porch of the rooming house where we lived, her head leaned back to point her face into the sun, her eyes closed. That's when I noted a striking resemblance between her and Joseph Stalin (a photo of Stalin in his funeral casket had appeared in the news recently). Without thinking, I mentioned this to her. She seemed genuinely hurt by the insinuation that she looked like the Soviet dictator. That was the only time I ever saw her betray any vulnerability.

She quickly recovered her composure and treated it as a joke; however, I was miserable over what I had done and felt moved to do her bidding without objection for weeks afterwards. She, of course was very pleased with this turn of events.

8.

In addition to the women's hygiene items, we sold other "personal products" (as Camilla called them), like jock straps, men's trusses and condoms. Camilla cautioned me against trying to handle a sale of such items because of my lack of experience and familiarity with the more "grown up" uses of these things. She instructed me to refer all such customers to her to handle.

Of course, I was chomping at the bit to get into the adult stuff, and I begged her to tell me what I needed to know in order to handle such delicate transactions.

Well, she said, "For instance, if someone asked for condoms (which were kept in the pharmacy room at the back of the store where the sight of them wouldn't embarrass the more genteel customers) I should first ask them what size they wanted, then go check the stock in the pharmacy. She may have meant the quantity or package size, but that's not what I heard.

This didn't even sound strange to me since from the conversations of the guys I had overheard, all men were NOT created equal, and it made sense that had to be taken into consideration.

So, naturally, the first time I had the opportunity to wait on a condom customer, I remembered to ask the right question.

It was just before closing time on a Saturday night, nobody in the store but Kenneth the pharmacist and me who was in the back counting pills, or whatever he did back there. Two boys about 17 or 18 came in and furtively asked for a package of Golden Knights. Weeeelll, I thought, here we go. I can do this! So, I asked the magic question: What size would you like?

A look came on both faces that I think can best be described as "terror" or maybe it was just extreme disbelief. At any rate, they took their bright red faces and fled. Left me standing there thinking how wimpy they were.

But then, I realized Kenneth had heard every word. He didn't seem to know what to do about it: be angry? Or just laugh like hell? Finally, he said, "well, I think we just need to close up and get to heck out of here on that note!"

But, he did report it to Mrs. Randall who on Monday when I came to work called me aside and barely suppressing her laughter, said, "Next time, Dorothy, why don't you ask them to come to the back and try on a few until they find their correct size."

9.

Camilla's real specialty was instructing me about men and sex. We lived in a run-down apartment building where most, if not all, of the tenants were students like us.

There were six units on the second floor where we lived and all of us shared one bathroom.
The unit directly across the hall from us was occupied by either three or four young guys. It was hard to tell which ones actually lived there because of so much coming and going. It seemed to be the headquarters of a small band who frequently practiced there. (Incidentally, one of the boys who spent time there was Roger Miller, THE Roger Miller!)

In view of this situation, Camilla saw fit to warn me that I should be very careful when using the bathroom. She said that I must always be sure to use only my own towels and washcloths because if I used a cloth one of them had used, it was possible I could get pregnant. She claimed to have known of just such a case where this actually happened.

Now, in truth, I was skeptical of that one, and I mentioned it to a few other girls school and asked what they thought. I got some strange looks from some of them, but in general, the consensus was a sort of "No."

I didn't argue with Camilla about it but I certainly made sure I never even touched a wash cloth that wasn't mine. Truth or not, I thought, no need to take chances.

10.

At the end of my first year at that school, I married my boyfriend and the next year we had a son.

Camilla came to the Delivery Room at the hospital when he was born to "help" me through my ordeal, though she had not the slightest notion of what giving birth meant. The story of her "helping" me through childbirth is told in another story which, maybe, I will tell you next year.

I did name my son after Camilla, by giving her last name to him as his middle name. Shortly afterward I moved away and we didn't see much of each other through the years. She married a very ordinary country boy, had three children, and died in her forties from breast cancer,

But, she left her mark on all of us who knew her.

Twenty five years later I moved back to that town to practice law and become the municipal judge. One night at a civic affair, a graying man with a nicely trimmed mustache whom I recognized as one of those boys who had lived across the hall, approached me at the buffet table. With a smile, he said, "Tell me, Dorothy, did you ever tell your boy that his daddy was a wash rag?"

NATURAL SELECTION

Before dictaphones & tape recorders
before reel-to-reel, before typewriters,
before computers, before laptops,
before iPads, before iPods,
there were women.
Take a letter, Miss

Scientists don't know it but
women have a direct connection
between their ears and their fingers.
No need to pass through the
wrinkled suet of the brain
the words crackle through auditory canals
imprinting on the wax lined passages
travel down, down through the arms
in their creamy skin speckled with freckles
along small shapely fingers
and spill onto the page
in perfect order.

STENOGRAPHY

The words entered my ears like bees buzzing
on a lazy afternoon. They flowed down my arms,
through my blind fingers, spilled onto the snowy
paper moving delicately like a spider traversing a gossamer
web. The wrinkled fabric of my brain
took no notice whatsoever of these mundane activities.

My imagination filled the walls of my skull
with my own words looking for a way out
of their bone prison

Fifty years of that before I released the prisoners
And let the words spill out on the pages as poems

They are the dangling threads that memory
can latch onto when everything else goes blank.

THE WORK OF DISCOURSE

As long as I can remember, I have heard the call
to speak for others. Standing no higher than the cradles
I rocked, I thought to interpret the bubbling sounds
of ones hardly smaller than me in whose charge
they were placed merely because I was oldest.

Later, standing to answer the haughty pedagogues who
cowed my youthful peers, I took the discipline that was
meted out for speaking as if authority was mine.

In maturity, moved to stand before the bench of judgment,
to argue, to plead on behalf of those whom the sovereign
would chastise or deprive, I found strength in my voice.

Now I do presume to say words in verse, in pentameter
and metaphor. My destined work is a conversation
with the world that comes to me through all my ancestry.

HONEST WORK

I never dreamed of being a high rise, striped tie attorney at
law. No. My dreams carried me back to a place like my
hometown. A version of Spoon River, where I solved
problems for farmers, hairdressers, waitresses, old women
bamboozled by magazine salesmen, harried wives trying to
escape a drunkard, his barroom brawls and fathering of
children. A country lawyer, maybe a female Atticus Finch.

My first practice was in an old barber shop on Main Street
in a ragged panhandle town, one barber chair left up front
visible from the street, bait for the lanky farmers
and cowboys who favored this manly furniture.

Harley Russell, toothless and calloused, the first to come
inside, couldn't resist propping manure caked boots on the
footrest
and pouring out stories like water from an artesian well.
He wanted a potion to keep his worthless son in law from
squandering his hard won pastures and cattle herd after
Harley's bones had been turned under. He liked what I did
for him. Angle parked pickup trucks soon lined the block.

The old country lawyer in the next town gave me these words:
Little lady, he said, *write as many $35 wills as you can, then
take extra good care of yourself and outlive them. Their
widows will hire you to probate their estates.* Good advice.

I drafted last wills and testaments for all comers: relatives,
neighbors, strangers who wandered too near the one-time

barber shop. I examined abstracts, memorized the Uniform Commercial Code, negotiated oil and gas leases, sued magazine salesmen, ripped the ass off the drunken husband. I burned the midnight oil, showed up on time, kept at it until the widows learned they could trust me and the men forgot I was a female.

This poem appeared in the anthology, *Raising Lilly Ledbetter: Women Poets Occupy the Workface,* edited by Carolyne Wright and M. Lyons (Univ. of Washington Press)

TESTOSTERONE BLUES

*Observations made while hanging
out down at the courthouse*

Hard-bodied, hard-boiled men with an air
of authority, betraying no sign of softness,
they stride the halls of power, stiff collared
and cuffed, serge stretched tight shoulder
to shoulder, in their mirror-toed wingtips,
and brush cuts.

A cloud of harshness lingers in their wake
wherever they go, invoking the faint sound
of drums, bugles, and hob-nailed boots,
sending a shiver of sadness through me
as I remember what Margaret Atwood said:
*Men are afraid women will laugh at them,
and women are afraid men will kill them.*

This poem first appeared in *Red River Review*
May 2015 Issue

OF BLIND PIGS AND ACORNS

I was a country lawyer for more than forty years, the first
woman lawyer to enter some of the old courthouses scattered
along the edge of the Great Plains. I was elated to be where I
was, to set foot into a world of men where "important
business" was being conducted and dramatic events were
happening. Everyone did not share my elation. One judge
shook his shaggy white head when I came before him, and
then deliberately and arrogantly mispronounced my name.
When I won my first jury trial in his courtroom, he said loudly
enough for all present to hear, including the jury, "Well, I
guess even an old blind sow finds an acorn now and then." I
smiled sweetly, nodded ever so slightly toward him . . . as if
he had uttered a compliment. I would not let his attempt to
humiliate me dampen my pleasure of victory. Almost every
interaction I had with him for almost thirty years carried the
same misogynist tone. Thorny, annoying, unnecessarily rude.
I retired from practicing law a few years ago and now have a
lot of fun trying to become a poet. Sometimes I miss the
lawyering, but not often. I certainly don't miss the misogyny.

Not long ago I walked into a cafe in the town where the old
judge lives since his own retirement and heard someone call
my name. I turned and saw a withered, crippled old man
hobbling along on a walker. Had he not called out in his
familiar voice, I would not have recognized the wrecked
person I saw before me. He looked more like a cadaver than
the arrogant judge of former days. As I approached him, he
said, "Well, what are you doing these days?" He even
pronounced my name correctly.

Our long history flashed like lightning through my mind and I
thought of the perfect reply. But, I caught myself and
consciously refrained from saying, "Oh, just scooping up
acorns, Your Honor. Bushels of acorns."

WORDS & CONSEQUENCES

At counsel table, in the midst of a trial, the absurdity
of what is happening flashes through my mind like a strobe
light. A woman sits beside me, accused of an act that if
proven will take away her life as she knows it. She will be
taken against her will to a place where she does not want to
live, but she will have no choice in the matter. She will sleep
in a small space where she is told to sleep, she will rise
when she is told to rise, she will eat what someone tells
her to eat, she will do work at someone else's bidding.

And whether this happens to her or not depends on
the words that come from my mouth when I stand to speak
on her behalf. Not just the words themselves, but how
I say them. The tone of my voice. My demeanor when
I say the words. All my actions, the way I rise from my chair,
the way I walk toward the box where the twelve sit,
the way I answer when the one sitting at the high desk speaks
to me. The way I search each face of the twelve. The way
I meet the gaze of each set of eyes. I must convey sincerity.
No whining, no bullying overtones. All this will color her life
from this day forward.

Each time I stand to question a witness, to importune
the judge, or to plead this woman's case to the jurors,
I must measure every movement no matter how slight,
every sound I make. It is a performance with more
consequences than the applause on a theatre stage.

But, I must not think on that in the thick of trial.
I must pull myself back into the moment.
I must listen intently to the story I am telling,
the music of the words I utter. I must create nuances,
gage the sounds that reach the ears of my listeners,
catch the vibrations they send back to me.

Timing is crucial if I am to become one with my audience,
as I am doing at this moment . . . as if survival,
mine, as well as hers, depended on it . . . which it does.

Each time I do this I feel as if I have received a measure
of forgiveness, if not outright redemption.

I consider myself the luckiest person to ever walk on this
spinning ball of dirt and ice!

4.
AND, THEN

ARS POETICA

It could have happened like this:

Music playing on the radio, her bare feet
starting to move, or, the sound of a dog
barking, distantly all through the night.

Was it the funeral of the old woman
she had loved always, who told stories
that would never leave her?

Perhaps it was how her mother bent
in the coming twilight to trim the lamp wick,
to polish the globe, to shoo out the dark.

Could it have been the first time she heard
the slow breath of love, warm and soft as a dove
cooing on a pillow beside her own head?

Suppose it was the sense of shadow
that followed her from the first time
she saw a slow black hearse on the road.

Neglected, abused, ignored, it never retreated,
though it did sleep at times.

It endured and grew until it announced itself
a miracle and began to behave like one.

OBSESSION

A ragged piece of paper began following me
about the time I learned to walk, but before
I learned to write. It begged me to make
marks on it that others could read. It followed
me everywhere. It threatened, it cajoled, it made
promises. I feared it, but was   obsessed by it.
I still am . . . both fearful and obsessed by
the making of marks on paper that I thrust
at others hoping they will read what I have written.

DEAR EDITOR

I am a late-coming poet
an old biddy who scratches
for words along the road

Not an academic
not a professional
nor an Iowa workshopper
My arrogance is home grown
and handmade

Still, I am a poet
and this what I call poetry

WORK AND MEMORY

Work is
a job,
an occupation,
a profession,
a vocation,
an avocation,
a sense of purpose
a conversation with the world

Now let us speak to loss and laissez-faire
And, finally, of mortality
of the striving to defy inevitability:
a cessation of thought and life.
And make an attempt at immortality

Memory is the guardian of all things,
So said Cicero, or whoever penned the
Rhetorica ad Herennium, along with
Aristotle, Bruno and Isadore of Seville.
Now, even the hoi polloi agree, and all
of us have a go at the Philosophers Stone.

We have to enlist the art of storytelling,
Weaving narratives of immortality that
lift us beyond the abyss over which the cradle rocks
as we amble along the dimly lit corridors
of existence until at our work here is done.

We have lived to tell the story,
And tell it, we must. Else, why are we here?

ASSIGNATION

for my soul mate, Devey Napier

If you saw it now, you might think it merely
a cheap room in a Panhandle cow town
huddled between Teresa's Mexican Kitchen
and Moody's Livestock Supply. You might render
a harsh judgment on the black plastic veneer
of bed and dresser, its faux gold trim. You might
go so far as to call it tasteless, tawdry, and point out
suspect stains on the bedspread, rust streaks
in the bathtub, sticky spots on the carpet.

But deities favor such lowly places and here
on a sultry afternoon, the small god of perfect
love decreed a shift in the molecular structure
of the universe and formed a perfect sphere. Here
two ragged souls mated and came home to live

She knew my dreams before I told them to her.
She echoed my grief for our lost children.
She warmed the frozen places in my secret life.

Meanwhile the drab room transformed into a fairy
tale. We plucked the yellow rays of light slicing
through the dirty windows like whetted blades,
and wore them as peacock feathers in our hair.

MY MOTHER'S WISHES FOR ME

My mother urged me at every opportunity to marry,
preferably some local boy, maybe the son of our nearest
neighbor. She wanted me to stay near where we could share
recipes, cook harvest dinners together, be housewives to our
farmer husbands. This refrain played in the background of all
my visits home until one Sunday morning as I was flying
toward Tokyo in a jumbo jet, and her heart gave up while
making breakfast for a half dozen of her grandchildren.

I never got around to telling her why I couldn't be her
housewife neighbor, that I wanted another woman for my
mate.

WEDDING VOWS

We never knew for sure where our love came from,
but we suspect it began in our yearning, perhaps
in the certain sadness and sorrows we had known,
we needed to find not meaning in loss, but ease from it.

Whatever we sought in the dark places where we lived,
we both knew on first meeting that the light had found
us, that comfort was at hand, if we had the courage to grasp it.
And, in truth, we married on that first day when we stood

together in the bright sunlight of a March day, and all
others, the world, receded into the distance leaving us
alone with this fortune that lay before us for the taking.
It seem we had walked toward this hour all our lives.

We never stood before an altar. We stood, first, in that
wooded glen and said the words that would bind us
in truth and in fact. Then, twenty years later, we faced
a magistrate, and somebody said "until death do us part."

Dorothy Alexander and Devey Napier were married in Santa
Fe County, New Mexico on October 28, 2013, after spending
the previous eighteen years of bliss together.

COMING OF AGE

At thirty I winced and vowed never
to acknowledge birthdays as limitation

At forty I perfected my swishy walk
to disguise the years roiling up in my wake.

At fifty I began to take long hikes
backpacking across whole continents

At sixty I joined a yoga group
and contorted myself backward twenty years

At seventy, I moved in ever longer strides
shoulders thrust back, breasts thrust forward

Now, at eighty, I embrace my age,
I grab it by the shoulders, kiss it on the mouth
thrusting my tongue in, bending all those years
backwards until we both fall down
laughing at all the nonsense we've been through

HER TATTOO

The faded lines lie on aging flesh
like the borders on an old map,
like blots dripped there by mistake,
smears of filmy blue and red.
How long ago did she live such a life?

The images are grainy and she must squint
to read the words criss-crossed by wrinkles.
A far cry from the tawny shoulder of that 1951
summer when the blunt needles spattered letters,
and a small red heart to emphasize sentiment
stitched into tender flesh.

No thought was wasted on questions of hygiene
or blood-borne plague by either the sidewalk artist
wiping excess blood and ink with his filthy rag,
or the recipient with tears streaming down her teenage
cheeks. Nor did she stop to consider her mother's
harsh judgment upon seeing the carnage.

She was beyond caution that crisp spring day
at the old State Fair Park on Eastern Avenue,
with all those young sailors calling out encouragement.

She could not foresee the years of taped covering,
the fortune paid to Johnson & Johnson, the embarrassed
excuses when others wore strapless nothings, not to mention
all the perjury committed when on forms she was asked
for *identifying marks* and wrote *none*.

CANNABALIZED

First, they took my tonsils.
I howled pitifully
—until the ice cream came.

Not long afterwards, they
came for my appendix.

Then, they took a cyst here,
an unspecified growth there,
not to mention the teeth,
one at a time at odd moments.

I swear there were times
they had a clipboard
checklist, crossing off
each item as they took it.

Hundreds of little vials
of blood, ingrown toenails,
warts, moles, fatty tumors,
bits for biopsies, gall bladder.
The whole reproductive
apparatus went out the door.

I feel like an old Chevrolet
no engine, no wheels,
rusting in a junkyard,
behind a wood fence
plastered with hubcaps
and a sign that says
Beware the Dog.

INVISIBLE WOMAN

She once turned heads as she passed
through the world. Her hair, her eyes,
her sleek body with curves and contours
like the gardens of Versailles, energy
emanating from her in atmospheric waves.

Now, of a certain age, she traverses the universe,
invisible to the naked eye, becoming smaller,
shrinking to nothing, in this world of youth,
in this place where all the young are blind.

This poem first appeared in *Red River Review*
May 2015 Issue

HOW TO GROW OLD

As I grow grayer and grayer
I know I don't have a prayer
of remembering my name
or how to play the game
but I do think I get
gayer and gayer.

BEEKEEPING

Emily heard a fly buzz when she died.
I say no flies for me. I want to hear
a busy bee buzzing his way back home,
flying low, weighed down with nectar,
work worthy of his reputed busyness.
I want to be buzzed by sweetness,
by elegant profit, a harvest of honeyed goodness,
by a worker who brings forth more than
this noisy fear of inadequacy that burdens
my own wavering flight, a thirst I would quench
for myself, if granted such power.

And as the earth dissolves like snow,
I want to see the Queen leading the procession,
her minions droning a dirge,
everything perfectly adequate at last.

WHEN THE TIME COMES

                              bury me deep,
and when I have been in the ground
for ten thousand years, I will still want
you beside me, in our warm bed, the dog
at our feet, you in my bones.
Even when I am turned to dust,
I will still want you.

DYING OF THE DAY

The sun lowers itself to the western edge of the world,
the heat subsides, now is the time for work
to ease itself down on its haunches, to slow the pace.
The men bring the horses to the corral where
a tank of cool water eases their burning thirst,
the day's labor ended for both man and beast.
Then the men lean against the porch rail
or sit on the benches under the elm trees,
roll cigarettes, shaking tobacco from flat red cans,
careful to distribute the flakes evenly, lick the paper,
twist the ends, draw a kitchen match against shoe
sole, and hold the sudden red flame to paper.
Inhale, exhale. All is done that can be done.
No regrets for this day or its end.
Time to go home.

LAST WORDS

Five miles this side of Texas lies a dusty family plot
of ground with a headstone bearing my name and birth
date. I will never see the second date carved on the stone.

Scorching summer sun burns and shrivels the buffalo grass
and wind blows incessantly in this place, bending cedar trees
into gray old men. They stand silently among the stones,
not out of reverence for the dead, or for their brave deeds
or honest lives, since death renders all such things irrelevant.
They stand silent because there's not a damn thing left to say.

ABOUT THE AUTHOR

Dorothy Alexander is a poet, storyteller and editor/publisher of a small independent poetry press that has published the work of fifteen finalists and five grand prize winners of the Oklahoma Book Awards for Poetry during the past ten years. She is the author of four poetry collections, including *Lessons from an Oklahoma Girlhood,* a collection of poems incorporating the art of twenty Oklahoma women artists. Dorothy is a founding member of the Woody Guthrie Poetry Group at the annual Woody Guthrie Folk Festival in Okemah, Oklahoma. She currently curates a monthly poetry reading at the Paramount Theatre in Oklahoma City. Much of her work is inspired by the agrarian literary tradition and the populist political movements of the early 20th Century in the United States. She embraces primarily the narrative form, what she calls "narcissistic" narrative, and she often indulges in "selfie" poetry.

Her work has appeared in Malpais Review, Blood & Thunder: Musings on the Art of Medicine, Cooweescoowee Journal and other media, and has been anthologized in *Times They Were A'Changing: Women Remember the 60s & 70s* (SheWrites Press), *Raising Lilly Ledbetter* (Lost Horse Press), *Women Writing Nature* (Sugar Mule Press) and others. The Oklahoma Center for the Book selected Dorothy as recipient of the Carlile Distinguished Service Award for her services to the Oklahoma literary community in 2013.

CPSIA information can be obtained
at www.ICGtesting.com
Printed in the USA
FFOW01n0308190615
14413FF